S0-BBB-655

HEALING THE
WOMANHEART

For Dottie Lou —

With love and deep gratitude
for your abiding friendship
with my Mama. May our
family feelings continue to
connect us all over time and
miles, and may these poems
bring you hope
and healing.

Monza
7-8-99

POEMS BY
MONZA NAFF

WYATT-MACKENZIE PUBLISHING

Some poems in this collection were previously
published in *Bay Windows, Common Lives/Lesbian
Lives, Diotima, Fugue,* and *Radiance.*

Wyatt-MacKenzie Publishing
15115 Highway 36, Deadwood, Oregon 97430
toll free 1-877-900-9626
www.WyMacPublishing.com

Designed by Nancy Cleary, www.designscapestudio.com
Set in Garamond Book. Printed on 80# Ivory Synergy Laid
Printed and bound at Eugene Print, Eugene, Oregon

Copyright ©Monza Naff 1999
All Rights Reserved.

F I R S T   E D I T I O N

Library of Congress Cataloging-in-Publication Data

Naff, Monza
        Healing the womanheart : poems / by Monza Naff.
        – 1st ed.
        p. cm.
        LCCN: 99-64205
        ISBN: 0-9673025-0-1

        1. Spiritual healing–Poetry. 2. Women–
Poetry. I. Title.

PS3564.A34H43 1999   811'.54
                          QBI99-901

HEALING THE
WOMANHEART

Also by Monza Naff

Exultation: A Poem Cycle in Celebration of the Seasons

FOR **SHARON**

ACKNOWLEDGMENTS

As I complete this book, I think of mentors, friends, and students who have encouraged and supported me in every phase of this collection's development, and I feel abundantly blessed. Thanks from this womanheart

❖ to Susan Cook, Mary Ann Klausner, and Dr. Gisela Bergman, who helped me take my life and my voice seriously;

❖ to Nancy Louise and Jamie Grace King, who pushed me to practice what I teach, to write down and read aloud what I had held inside for twenty years;

❖ to my support group – Virginia Filley, Carole Jackson, Jane Mara, Shirley Miller, Maggy Rose, Barbara Baird, Mary Hagedorn, and Kris Kennedy – who held on to the lifeline;

❖ to Mary DeShazer, Ozzie Mayers, Anne Leonard, S. Mara Faulkner, Pema (Nancy Clark) and Yeshe (Caroline Parke), Marilyn Farwell, the late Izzy Harbaugh, Katherine Witteman, Mary Schlotter, Susan Bausserman, Nancy Parker, Jill Christman, Judy Voruz, Linda Rice, Liz Dooley, Tiare Mathison-Bowie, Barbara Pope, and C. Anne Laskaya, who have believed in me across the continent, have given careful response to my work, or urged me to "go public";

❖ to my Writing Groups in Eugene – Jean Besson, Jill Christman, Kate lyn Hibbard, Mary Hotchkiss, Jamie Grace King, Myeba Mindlin, and Val Rapp; in Portland – all the 29th Street Writers; at Flight of the Mind (1990-1998); and here in Oakland – Mary Hidalgo, Meg Quigley, and Roussel Sargent, all of whom have helped me grow poems;

❖ to my students at the University of Oregon and in workshops around the country, who kept asking me to read my work to them;

❖ to my companions in the "Creative Writing and the Inner Life" classes I facilitate in Oakland, who constantly stimulate my creative impulses;

❖ to my teachers – Marjorie D. Lewis, Elizabeth Woody, Judith Barrington, Ursula Le Guin, Evelyn C. White, Toi Derricotte, and Mimi Khalvati – who have given me sustaining guidance, critique, and support;

❖ to Judith Barrington and Ruth Gundle, who have created the extraordinary environment of Flight of the Mind, a summer writing workshop for women;

❖ to Nancy Cleary, my publisher, whose vision, energy, and faith in this book and me have been surpassed only by her steadfast friendship, which I cherish.

❖ to my family of origin – especially Mama (Rose Mary Fishback), Dad (Walter R. Naff) and Jayne, my sister, Debra Naff Dacus, and brother-in-law, Brent – for rich material and so much love;

❖ to my family of friends here in Oakland, who always want to hear what's hot off the printer – Jennifer Biehn, Joan Lohman, Vicki Dello Joio, Sherry Mouser, Michael Bell, Ann Jauregui, Nancy Thompson, and Kostas Bagakis;

❖ to Judith Cope, who first made a book out of my stacks of paper and called it a joy, whose friendship brings a thousand graces to my life;

❖ to Ami Atkinson, who has given me immeasurable gifts by allowing me to be her mother, has mothered me as well in countless ways, and who loves to read as much as I do; and to my son-in-law, Jesse Combs, who has truly become a son to me, a scientist who gives sensitive response to my very non-scientific work;

❖ and, finally, to Sharon Ellison, my partner in life, tireless listener, astute critic, and constant ally, because of whom my heart is healing.

TABLE OF CONTENTS

**I :
CLAIMING THE LEGACY**

II:
EXPOSING THE ILLUSIONS

III:
HEALING THE WOMANHEART

I :

CLAIMING THE LEGACY

At Three

At three, I lived with shadows.
In our living room on Green Street
every night my parents studied,
bent silhouettes in lamplight,
while I lay nearby on the couch, my bed,
drifting, gliding, in and out,

floating on waves of sleep and words,
leaving, then listening again.
When they tiptoed out past midnight
and closed the bedroom door,
I lay in sudden silence cold and grey,
watched reading chairs and standing lamps,

oak dining table and Ming vase
all cease to be themselves.
Afraid to open, too curious
to close my eyes, I saw shadows come alive.
Shadows always crawled behind thick bars
from streetlights filtered through venetian blinds,

casting charcoal strips across the walls
while cicadas flung themselves against the screens.
These shadows crept, grew into giant hands
with baseball bats for fingers,
then shrank to baby hands
with fingers small as birthday candles.

Faces peered right through those bars:
kitten eyes, daddy's mama's eyes;
mouths as big as whales,
then small as goldfish gaped in O's;
noses flared with tunnel nostrils,
shriveled into dolly noses, stiff and small.

I hugged my Teddy, curled my finger
through the hole in his soft bear neck
to feel the comfort in the stuffing lumps.
For hours I breathed shadows behind bars,
stretch and shrink, stretch and shrink,
over and over in time with my heart.

Magic

Grandma of the golden raisins
built a castle out of dough,
bought the mudpie bakery goods,
then put on a puppet show.

Grandma of the tapioca
pulled the taffy into string,
wove a garland out of roses,
made the old piano sing.

Grandma of the Maida stories
rocked the pale girl 'neath the moon,
charmed the passing ships to harbor,
then sailed over sea and dune.

Grandma of the trilling whistle
coaxed the owl into her hand,
spoke by heart a thousand poems,
sent the girl home magic, tanned.

Roses from her Rage

the fierce and flaring garden you have made
out of your woes and expectations
tilled into the earth
         - Adrienne Rich, *"Contradictions: Tracking Poems"*

My grandmother grew roses from her rage.
She tilled her shrill, sharp tongue,
her gossip, judgments, and despair into the earth
and the ground gave thorns.
Out of her sadness, loneliness, and yearning
she cultivated compost that gave rise
to a hundred shades of color I see still;
delicious smells arose, some pungent, others soft,
and beautiful, melodic sounds hovered in the air:
"Coronation," "Peace," "Savannah," "Everlasting."
I held her hand and tiptoed through that plot of earth,
so unaware at nine that I was treading on
the "fierce and flaring garden" of her life.
I only felt her love of roses, pressed into my palm.

Icons
   - for Debbie

Shh, baby sister. Listen, precious. We have to
whisper. You have to behave. Never laugh in
church. It's not OK. Yes, you can smile; smiling's
good. Shh, listen. Always sit still, still as an oak pew.
Look alive while Daddy preaches even if you're
reading comics or making jokes out of the titles in
the hymn book (yeah, I know, shh, "Love Lifted Me"
is "the skirt song," now shh). Stop it, I'm serious,
you're shaking the pew even if you are laughing
without making a sound. Shh, now, listen. If you
get the hiccups, especially during communion, hold
your breath and count to 20, and never ever burp
or fart, pop your gum, or click your pen. Don't give
those ladies something to talk about. Shh, be quiet,
Mama's busy. She's up there playing the organ, see?
Listen, listen. Be still, still as a pulpit. When the
ushers pass the offering, take the plate and pass it
even if you can't find your quarter to put in right
then; no, you can't take change. Shh, Dub, listen,
listen. Let's play tic-tac-toe; shh, you can be either
X or O. Don't talk to Sydney, stop it now, no, not
even a whisper, not when the choir sings; yes, I
know that Pearl McKinney's teeth click and she
sings off-key; yes, it is funny. Shh, I mean it, listen to
me. Don't swing your legs. Just be still, please, still
as a marble altar. Don't swish your petticoats even
if they're scratching the back of your legs, and don't

stare at the woman nursing her baby in the next
row; the baby's head is under the blanket so you
won't gawk at her mother's you know whats.
Shh, you've got to listen. Don't pick your nose, and
no don't blow your nose so loudly. That man's
scowling at you. Just be still, still as a stained glass
window. Share your hymn book with the woman
over there. I know she smells funny, do it anyway.
Yes, you may lean against me, yes you may take a
nap, but don't spread all out now. We have to set
a good example. People watch us. Shh, listen. No,
you can't go to the bathroom unless you absolutely
can't hold it; it's got to be a real emergency. You
have to plan ahead, go just before and again right
after. That's what I do. Shh, precious, listen, listen.
For this hour, for this one hour, please be still, still
as a gold candlestick.

A Bird In A Child's Hands

My sophomore year in college
had a difficult beginning –

leaving home one late summer morning at eight
for campus, off to lead orientation tours,
saying an offhand "good-bye" to my mother,
who was vacuuming, coming home at noon
to her note – "I've gone to think things out" –
her clothes gone from her closet.

I stayed at home that year I was nineteen,
mothering my father and thirteen-year-old sister,
keeping house, working two jobs,
taking twenty-one hours a term in school,
trying to love a man, trying to love a woman –
unaware of anger, only sadness, deep grief.

One afternoon in the late winter I took off work,
went window shopping along Berry Street,
not far from campus. A little gift shop on a
side street drew me in – no kitsch in the windows.
Crystal, brass, marble, silver – delicate, enduring
works of art, all beyond my means.

My eyes riveted on a marble sculpture
of a child holding the bird in her or his
tiny, sturdy hands. I saw reverential awe,

curious delight in the child's face
for the fragile bird – a wren, a baby sparrow –
that would trust a human hand.

That day marble spoke, stone talked.
I wanted that sculpture to live with me,
to be my icon. Only money stood in my way.
I went back to that shop off Berry Street once a week
for several months, scanning all the merchandise
but really only looking at the child and bird.

Each time I pushed the sculpture back to some
obscure place on the shelf, securing it, saving
money out of each check. When I finally had enough,
I stuffed the cash in my pocket, walked to the shop.
Inside, I gave up the facade of shopping, went straight
to the shelf where my sculpture was. It was gone.

I looked everywhere in the shop,
stomach wrenching, eyes filling, heart pressing.
Suddenly the owner came in from the
storeroom, holding my sculpture.
She handed it to me, her eyes shining.
"I saved it for you," she breathed.

Louder, but still softly, she murmured,
"A few days ago a woman came into the store,

looked at the piece for a minute, and said
'I guess it'll do.' I couldn't let her take it.
So I told her I'd sold it and forgot to mark it."
I had never said a word to that shopkeeper

about the child and bird, only "thank you"
every week as I left. That was all I said that day
after she wrapped the piece in tissue, put it in a box,
and I paid. I have had that sculpture in every one of the
thirteen places I've lived since I was nineteen.
I unpack it, set it on a table, and I'm home.

Self-Portrait I*

I cannot:
sew
send gifts on time
write letters hardly ever
make phone calls to strangers
walk into parties alone without pain
engage in small talk with someone I don't know
wear a bikini

I cannot
stop:
worrying
biting my cuticles
spending energy on guilt
eating tortilla chips once I start
believing that I need my parents' approval
rushing, taking stairs two at a time, driving fast
thinking that I should be able to wear a bikini

I can:
cook almost anything, anywhere
laugh until I cry nearly every day
create a party with no money for any reason
smile at crying children and have them smile back
walk into an unfamiliar kitchen and find any gadget or spice
get more excited over other people's triumphs than my own
wax my car, slowly, with a bikini.

*In the manner of Tove Ditlevsen, Danish poet

After

After I put the brown sugar on the oatmeal
        before the milk, gave a hardboiled egg
to the postman, walked far away from my
        high hill, whichever way you look at it,
I asked, "Who's empty? Who's crooked?"
        and all I could see were her sweet hands, the
road back to them broken, rolling like a river.

Menu

The menu of the day is posted
in the stairwell of the building
where I teach - in air,

wafting up the flights
from refectory to classrooms
high above.

I climb the stairs
and know that breakfast features
bacon, coffee cake, rolls of cinnamon

and raisins, and lunch will offer
fish sticks, tacos, and a pudding -
maybe butterscotch - for just desserts.

Later, when I descend
I know that dinner
will bring sauerkraut -

a reuben sandwich underway? -
or maybe German sausage with potatoes
and a chocolate cake.

When I smell a turkey roasting,
I know that harvest home is near.
I feel at home more in that stairwell

than any other place I go. The kitchen
comes to classroom as I climb the stairs.
In my mind I hear the women

talking, stirring, sifting, tasting
and I'm once again a child
who's coming home to love.

The Old Ones

Funny how the old ones let their secrets slip.
You may be canning peaches, making cherry pies,
or quilting at the table, eating apple crisp,
when Great Aunt Virginia, 88, begins to weep.

"What's wrong, Auntie Ginny?" "Oh, never mind me."
"It matters to me," you say, cupping a hand over her
inflamed knuckles and looking her square in the eyes.
"Mmm . . . sometimes I'm back in that orchard."

What orchard? You wait, gather crumbs from the table,
she smoothes out the folds in her apron.
"It was in that orchard in Yakima when
that ol' cousin Frankie, always such a randy cuss,

took us kids pickin'. We was takin' a break
and messin' around - it was a long time ago,
what's the use?" But by now Mama and Ruby have
turned around from the stove or away from their patches

and the room is completely still.
All ears are on Aunt Ginny. "He grabbed me
to tickle, I guess, and we got to wrestlin' - I was ten
and a tomboy - I liked to wrestle - but, well

Frankie never liked to lose, so he pinned me
face down under the ladder, right near our buckets
of fruit. He huffed in my ear while he yanked
on my drawers, but I kept laughin' 'cause I thought

he was teasin', just gonna play-whip my bare butt
like Daddy with his switch. But then Frankie
put his big ol' cherry-stained hand up there and
split me like a wishbone." She adds in a whisper,

"I heard it crack. My face was down in that
orchard dirt, and I couldn't hardly breathe."
She sighs, "It's the smell of the fruit, I guess,
sometimes gets me."

Still Lives

- for Mimi Khalvati

In the city in her peach and blue flat
the woman studies a volume of Goethe,

remembers last summer's blustery day
at the lake with her six best friends,

watches the finch stir in its wicker cage,
orange anemones stretch from their pot

yet still hears the pine tree, their picnic
of tea, grapes, and cheese in the sun.

She takes the pair of silver shears
from the desk, cuts herself out of her life,

tapes herself again to the sand, naked,
wringing out her long, wet hair,

pours Darjeeling into the paisley china cup,
meditates on her card bearing "Nord - Sud,"

sees the comfortable breasts of her friends,
in windblown silence by the sailboat, bobbing.

In the city, under the finch's watery song,
the woman recites Goethe, smelling ripe pears.

In the Curve of Your Brow

In the curve of your brow,
the full curve of your brow,
the curve of your full brow,
your full brow, your full, full brow,
your wide full window, your wall,
your whisper, your wisdom, your wish,
sight, wish your sight, fir sight,
fir, fir, fir, fir tall, fir tall tall,
fir tall in the woods, in the dark woods,
in the dark cool woods, in the peace,
in the peace, in the soft, soft peace,
in the soft, in the soft soft safe,
in the safe of your love, your dear love,
you're safe, safe, Love, I see love,
see you, want you safe
in the curve of your brow.

Black Snag

When it was over,
we divided linens, lamps and pans,
claimed gifts intended to be shared,
picture, vase, Ukrainian egg,
took back books that for ten years
had slept together.

Packing, I memorized each room,
heard the conversations, moans, and rhythms
of our bodies in quilts, our work in desks
and reading chairs, sounds embedded in the walls,
and forged indelible the vista from each window
as if warned I would go blind.

When I left that day,
I looked up and away, not back or ahead,
recited, "jezo hondo spruce, broadleaf maple,
forsythia, red tipped photinia," saw a skein of geese
fly in their primal V and a red hawk
survey the hill from a black snag.

That Fire

Sorrow is not the worst.
The worst are memories of anger,
fire that licks and catches,
feeding on the thrown spaghetti,
broken glasses and platters,
torn pages of a favorite book,
clothes strewn down the driveway,
words screamed through closed windows,
a pantomime of hate.
That fire leaves nothing
but ashes in its path,
and it never retreats.

For Maggie*

"Go easy, old friend," I whispered, and you did.
We stood by, weeping, as you crossed over
into the land of wild ones that late afternoon.
Three deer awaited you in the woods of home, and
I believe they met you, introduced you to the clan
as the new cat crone, a wise one, familiar with their ways,
once I planted you at nightfall beneath the maple tree,
the only sadness I ever planted in that soil.
I wailed, they watched, the cycle went round.
The crocuses were blooming, and the moon was full.

*Maggie was a Siamese cat who died at the age of 20. I had
known her half my life. My friend, Marilyn, and I had shared
life with her for years and shared her death on the 20th of
February, 1989. She is buried in the land she claimed as hers
in the hills of southeast Eugene, Oregon.

Blue Moths

While we had our tea our sadness circled the kitchen
as if a jar of blue moths had been let out to spin across
the room.

– Alice Hoffman, *Angel Landing*

The tea in my cup smells of peaches and spice
yet tastes like ashes, runs like bloody water
when I recall in my spring warmed kitchen

Mama's perfume clinging in hallway air
for days after she left, her clothes stripped from closets,
the note saying only "I've gone to think things out"

the amplified confusion in David's phone booth voice when I said
I couldn't marry him, knowing without knowing why that if I'd leave
Sara to cleave to him I'd risk a vital loss, be homesick for myself

my old cat Maggie's eyes as they turned
from trusting mirrors to cold marbles
as she died at my command that winter day

Dulcina's strong voice sounding from a spent shell
as she smiled that final time, saying, "Well, wherever I go now,
my hands and feet won't be cold anymore."

Blue moths nibble, flutter,
          hover near the heartflame,
                spin.

Over and Over

Over and over.

What is the pulse of a star?
What is the beat
of hydrangeas' breath?

The river runs over.

How can I breathe like a tree –
from my finger leaves, my roots –
live in a measure slow as death?

The river runs over
the moss-covered rock.

When is the thought of dahlia
stored somewhere in this bulb
all year until its season?

The moss-covered rock.
Over and over.

Where do the whales sleep
in the Pacific?
How do they know when to stop?

Over the river.
The rock.

Why did you die, Cara?
Why did you die?
Why did you die that way?

Over and over
the river runs over
the moss-covered rock.

II:

EXPOSING THE ILLUSIONS

Petroglyph Lake
   - *for my companions*

No fishin' here–this lake's dead.
   - A fisher to his grandson

Hear drums whisper in the lake bed,
alkaline and dry, where 10,000 people,
Paiute, Snake, and Klamath,
danced 8,000 years ago.

In obsidian chips, antelope prints,
herbivore teeth and sage,
watch ancient nightfires crackle
and smell roasting game.

Coyote slinks along the ridge;
shiver in the sun.

Read pathcodes in petroglyphs
carved above lava and bones.
Fat lizard faces west.
A bat, large caves.

In the stone above soft dirt
see an upside down stick man,
the spot of a grave
long since eroded, bones scavenged away.
Hear the keening, wailing.

Crouch down and touch three figures,
arms outstretched above their heads,
small circle at the right.
Stand one day away from healing.
Medicine wheel hides in mountain brush.

Veil

- *for Pema and Yeshe, in retreat*

Buddha is
behind a veil.
Spider web
filigrees across
wooden shrine
in Green Gulch garden.
Gauzy light
shines on God's face,
flickers, shifts
in shadow.
If Buddha is
behind a veil,
the veil is mind.

Phone Line

Three crows flew lazily
across lazuli bunting sky toward
the black phone line as dusk drew near,

swaggered news of exploits, territories won,
strained to claim their share of line, of air,
and preened sleek suits of ebony with purple tinge

while the line beneath their feet carried messages
of final offers, last hour deals, and mindless
clawing, cawing.

Blue River Laundromat
- *for Ursula*

I

I came to clean my clothes.
Black wrought-iron fish
swim on pale yellow walls.
Signs on a beat-up bulletin board
advertise aerobics at the Grange,
loving day care in Marie's home,
and Jason, the local handyman.

II

A shivering family – like
Papa, Mama, and two Baby Bears –
come in from a campground
beside the Blue River
where it rained last night.
Their sleeping bags are soaked.
"We only need a dryer," they sigh.
The kids are cranky as old Grizzlies.
I came to clean my clothes.
I read the morning paper.

III

A man who smells of old
bourbon and sweat throws his load,

unsorted, into the "Heavy Duty
Family Load" machine and asks us all,
"Think it'll ever stop rainin'?"
His eyes, swimming in beige water,
scan the want ads. He needs a job.
I came to clean my clothes.
I make a list of rivers I have known.

IV

A woman whose shoulders hold the smoke
of too many cigarettes and the cold of
too many rivers sorts her load,
his faded tan workclothes, her orange
polyester, their no-nonsense underwear.
She drinks Diet Pepsi and eats M & Ms.
She with shoulders of smoke and cold
watches fish swim in stained yellow seas.
She never says a word.
I came to clean my clothes.
I hum and count my quarters.

V

Outside the rain-streaked window
college students from New Jersey
burrow through a VW Bus, pulling

dirty clothes from duffel bags
and under the sagging seats.
Four of them rush in, laughing,
and yell, "Jesus, it's packed in here!
Any machines left for us?"
Papa Bear points and says, "Plenty."
I came to clean my clothes.
I remember writers on another river.

VI

A bearded man with a Budweiser belly
pushes through the door with a pink
hamper overflowing, shoves it onto
the counter painted robin egg blue.
His daughter or very young wife
takes over, sorts, and measures soap.
He shouts, "Hiya, Bill! How's it goin'?"
to the bourbon man weary of rain,
takes me in with a wink–
"How'd we get so dirty in a week, hunh!?"
I came to clean my clothes.
I watch my heart spin with the shirts.

If only

If only I had railed,

if only he had bellowed,
she had shrieked, I had stormed,

if only we had argued,
snarled, debated, and slammed doors,

if only they had yelled
instead of hissing behind walls,

if only we had pressed,
"Tell the secret! Fuck your shame!"

if only one had thrown
a chair, or broken plates or glass,

if only I had practiced
raging curses in a mirror

perhaps you would have never left,
she'd be sober, he, alive,

and anger wouldn't make me
vomit, disappear, or quake

if only I had railed.

No place to go

An old man feeds challah to the pigeons
at the corner of Lakeside and Grand –
"A bite for you, a bite for me," he sings.
He sits at the bus stop with no place to go.

Wisps of white hair curling beneath his
red wool stocking cap, his full white beard and
ruddy cheeks convince me, waiting for a light,
that Santa's come to Oakland in July.

The old man lives outside. He's dressed in ragged
layers of trousers, shirts – red, green, black, blue –
and lace-less, cracked brown boots with holes so big
his baby toes stick out, all caked with mud and oil.

Perhaps this man was captain of a fishing boat
in Alaska – or maybe it was Maine – or Oregon
until his wife left, and his heart did, too. Then
he wandered to the Bay and forgot his name.

But he keeps his Safeway cart well oiled,
the plastic bags hanging from its sides tied
with strong knots, his tarps all mended.
He's never forgotten how to tend his home.

And he vaguely remembers the gulls
circling over his head while he gutted salmon
when he feeds the pigeons and sings. I want
to call him by name. The light turns green.

Monday's First Appointment

He tells his side of the story:
He didn't hit her, his hand did.

I listen to him justify his rage,
disengage his person from her pain,
watch burning tar ooze behind his eyes,

razors sprout from all ten fingers,
spikes emerge from forehead, navel, arms,
fire spill through lips, over tongue,

his heart cower hidden, small and red,
while outside the window in the rain
a cat pounces on a varied thrush.

"Why do you think she's afraid?"

Who to Trust?

A boy, rifling through a car
at 4 a.m. on a dare, a prank,
sweat pearling on the soft
whiskers of his upper lip,
is shot, killed by the car's owner,
a law and order guy.

In court, the owner's acquitted
of any wrongdoing.
His teeth grind, jaws quiver,
and his right eye twitches
as his lawyer works the crowd.
"I didn't want to see anyone killed,"
the car owner says on the stand. "But you
don't know who to trust anymore."

A jury of neighbors,
as scared as he
of boys loose in the night,
do their duty.
No one looks
at the boy's mother.

Sanctus

I take my seat.
The board room is so cold
that the hairs on my arms stand soft.
A tribunal, the Commission on Ministry,
has convened to test my calling.

"In anticipation of our conversation regarding my re-licensure,
I am writing to let you know some of what I have been thinking
and praying about ... I have become aware that since my wedding
this past spring, my sexual orientation is a concern for you."

Holy, holy, holy

These people claim to be my friends.
I scan the room. Some have known me
all my life. Held me as a baby. Heard my
confessions, saw me baptized, stood with me
in healing circles, listened to my prayers.
I know them by their names,
know their families, too, hold many
of their secrets in my heart.

"I believe I live my life under holy orders. I know that I have been
called to be a spiritual teacher and guide, preacher, and ethical
catalyst. I will do my work in the world whether or not I am
licensed by this denomination."

They sit in judgment.
Yet they look afraid,
though they cannot understand
exactly why they fear me.
I watch them try to smile.

Holy, unholy, holy, unholy

I recite their names
inside my head and think,
"These people think they are my superiors.
Yet they've sought my guidance, asked my prayers,
for ten years used my talents."

God of power and might

Oh, God

"I have served as the chairperson for a regional commission,
developed new resources for spiritual renewal, facilitated dozens of
retreats, preached in several pulpits, including some of yours, offered
workshops at assemblies, and contributed my financial resources.
But I do not currently have a local church home."

The tribunal sets the rules.
"Why," asks the woman who drinks

in secret and needs everybody's approval,
the woman I've held in my arms as she wailed,
"don't you just go to church in your own town?
That's all we ask of you."

Heaven and earth are full of your glory

But this room is full of . . .

*"After five years of working in a local church I made the very
painful decision that I could no longer continue to participate in
a church where I was consistently negated and violated – as a
lesbian who needs to worship and study with my partner and
child in a spiritual community who sees us as one of the families
in the church, not one of the 'others'; as a feminist who sees
inclusive language in worship as a vital matter of theology, of
what is good news for women as well as for men; as an intelligent
woman who needs to be fed by intellectually and spiritually
challenging messages, music, and study, as well as social activities
that value who I am and what I have to offer."*

"These people are cowards," I whisper to myself.
"They refuse to look me in the eye.
They'd rather look for words to banish me,
and so they will. I am sorry they are so afraid."

Hosanna in the highest

How can I shout "Hosanna" here?

"Over the ten years I have ministered in this region, I have never hidden the fact that my partner in life is a woman, but I have not announced it either. Our wedding last spring resulted in that announcement. Choosing to have a public ceremony was the culmination of our individual and united efforts to be whole and honest, and I know that my work in the world, my ministry, is enhanced by my primary relationship, which is solid, healthy, and mutually challenging."

The Chairman repeats
the precise name and number of the rule:
Ministers in good standing
must worship in a local congregation.
He will not speak the word "lesbian,"
they will not talk about the real issues,
refer to my letter, which they have all read.

Blessed is the one who comes in Your name

"If there are those of you who question whether lesbians or homosexual men should minister among you, I would ask you to look again closely at the words of Jesus, who says nothing about who to love, but much about loving and about those who judge and hate.... Is it wise in this day when millions are desperate for the unconditional love of Jesus to refuse to let a willing servant share that healing presence in your name?"

Who, who are the blessed?

Members of the Commission
stare down at their notes,
smile at the rule book.
They disown me
from their family of faith.
I leave my seat.

Who has the right to rip blessing away?

*"... It would have been much easier to simply not reapply for
licensure or to apply and keep silent about the connection
between "standing" and where I stand as a whole daughter of
Christ.... But those would not have been the paths of wholeness
and of faith in the people of God to explore their true calling in
times of change and challenge. So I write to you in the spirit of
love, believing that if we discuss these issues in my situation,
we may be better prepared as a church for the others who
come to you with a clear, distinct calling and circumstances
that do not fit simplistic definitions. I am doing this for them
as much as for myself."*

I look at them one last time.
I smile, my eyes hold firm:
"I do not give you permission
to silence my voice."

Hosanna in the highest.

On Fence Posts

The red-tailed hawks perch on fence posts
beside the freeway this time of year.
And I think of the Church Fathers.

Stern and immobile, the hawks watch
the Cadillacs and Hondas fly past,
alert to swerving, someone breaking rules,

mistaking them for prey while mice nibble
through mint fields behind their backs.
Drivers watch the road and dream.

The red-tailed hawks have torn beaks,
shredded talons, lice-filled feathers,
and no one listens when they shriek.

"I dreamed I was Artemis . . ."

I ate men whole,
fell laughing on their shards of bone,
and picked my teeth with needles
after the feast.

Old Man

Old man, old man,
how does she tell the truth of you?

You shook her shoulder in the dark,
coaxed her awake and to the fishing hole
with oatmeal cookies, deviled ham,
and promises of rainbow trout by night.

Enroute you quoted Shakespeare,
taught her the alphabet in Greek,
and tutored her in Vaudeville acts
that you could both perform.

At river's edge she watched you gather
up the wicker creel, tackle box, and rods,
the reels, lunch, and lucky hats.
She hooked the worms for bait.

Catching a trout one time,
she slipped on moss,
then, soaked clear through,
stood shivering and brought the rainbow in.

But she also saw you with that boy
in the basement of the church,
pressing him against the table,
rubbing up against his jeans.

When she grew up, a man told her
you'd touched him "there" in sleep.
He dreamed his genitals were "stung"
and woke up "terrified of bees."

As years passed, others whispered
how you took them out to fish,
delighted them with jokes, old songs,
deep coffee-laced philosophy.

But under Cascade stars, they say,
your hands roamed, and they froze,
too scared to breathe or move.
Yet no one ever spoke of it at dawn.

Old man, old man,
How can she tell the truth of you?

Field of Vision

The reaper of grim thoughts returns
and cutting, cutting, comes across
my field of vision, mows me down –
in spite of purple iris and the snow,
your laughter and my vows to stand my ground.

I can't escape his scythe's harsh sound,
the sweeping, screeching in my heart
across my heath of hope, crushed low –
in spite of ocean waves, sunlight through firs,
your constant love and my vows to sing.

Yet I will plant again this spring,
believing, cleaving to the chance
that he'll surrender, impotent –
no match for laughter, iris, snow, and waves,
the sunlit firs, your love, and my firm vows.

For if the reaper, hacking boughs,
can, cutting, sweeping, screeching, kill
the meadow of one flowering life,
then part of this world's promise surely fades –
the joy, the wonder, passion, and the vows.

Nectarine
- *for Kostas*

The day I'd taught an old man to read,
    I ate a nectarine.
I met the man in the alley
        behind the University Bookstore.

I was moving again, hunting boxes.
    I asked the man,
"Do you have enough tarps?"
        It was raining. The guy looked cold.

He replied, "Yeah, I'm set –
        you need some?"
The man in the alley smiled.
        I felt embarrassed.

"That was a stupid assumption I made,"
        I said, looking him right in the eyes.
"Never mind, hon, you didn't mean nothin.
        We're all fucked."

He went on, "Here I'm hangin' by a bookstore,
        and I can't even read."
"Do you want to?"
        "Yeah."

"Well, I'll help you. Shall we go have
        some coffee and talk?"
We drank, the man told his story
        and asked me a lot about mine.

Every Monday, Wednesday, and Friday
        we worked for an hour at Espresso Roma.
He practiced in between, more than
        any of my students across the street.

In four months he could read the paper.
        It was June 4th
when he read it aloud to me.
        My coffee was iced. He was proud.

I smiled and shook his hand.
        When I left,
a man could read the paper
        and I ate a nectarine.

To My Students

We're on the edge of oceans,
dangerous waters,
you and I.

I know stagnation's smell,
I've felt the fear of undertow,
the tides, and sneaker waves.

I want to stretch our muscles,
not give balm for our inertia,
so I coach.

I shout instructions,
demonstrate, correct a posture,
hold you up, encourage and applaud.

You want to feel the current's power
and so we practice,
but I do not swim for you.

Suttle Lake 1990

They come to seek the stillness of a natural
place, and their way of seeking assures the
failure of their search.
                              – Wendell Berry

Damn you, Wendell, you're right.
You've got me pegged.

I come to find the stillness.
My foot pump hisses air
into a thick air mattress
to raise me off the ground.
The electronic ignition on my
propane stove and lantern
insures instant heat and light.
A plastic canopy over the picnic table
makes me impervious to rain
and the chaise lounge, now folded out,
is certainly more comfortable
for reading mysteries than a stump.

I do find rest in fleeting glimpse –
a perfect mirror of the mountain
in the lake at sunrise,
the awareness of no sound at night
save my lover's sleeping breath.
Yet I still hear dark trucks shift gears
and, worse, my own internal clatter.

Wendell, can't we talk this through?
Won't the demon at the gate still be my own?

A Crucible of Pain

"It was just a short emotional affair–
Not even physical. No harm done," they say.
"And, look, you learned a lesson, and besides,
your relationship survived." They do not see.

It was a crucible of pain for us. Held in its core,
as winter turned to spring, we felt the heat
of passion, rage, and anguish calcining our hearts;
all excess sloughed, our needs became refined.

Our metal took the hot assault, the flame,
and we emerged transformed. Melted then,
we each are tempered, more resilient, strong.
The bonds we forged have power to endure.

Translation

I wake to rain.
The flood of years rises
before my eyes: damp jackets
and jumpers, soaked socks,
dripping hair, the drizzle
at the doorstep, fumbling
with a key to enter dark houses,
living rooms where no one lived,
no one to talk to but a TV or
a cat, looking up from texts
at snaking water on glass.
Then all the words I think
are in the language of alone.
The chill of sorrow seeps
deeper than quilt can cover.

The woman I love still sleeps,
but when she wakes to rain,
she'll speak a different language,
talk of tuna sandwiches,
tomato soup, a game of Scrabble.
She'll whistle "We Three Kings"
and smile at every window.
She thinks of her mother,
the days they stayed at home
to listen to "The Shadow,"
read aloud from "Little House"

and play games by the fire
while water soaked the earth.

I climb out of bed,
pull on my sweats, thick socks,
chop some kindling, brew the coffee,
listen to Segovia play Bach
on his guitar, start a fire.
I look out the window,
practice smiling,
begin translation.

Reunion

I

"Thought you didn't love me anymore,"
she whispered, clinging to me
when she arrived.

"When you never wrote, I figured
you stopped loving your Gram."
She patted my face, wept.

"You was always my Doll,
my Angel Number One."

We face each other,
my back straight, hers stooped.
I have her eyes, her love of roses.

"Well, Gram, I guess I didn't understand.
You always groused at me, about my life.
I thought you didn't like me very much."

Her eyes brightened, grinned.
"Pshaw, that's just my way."

II

Papa was a saint, Mama was a whore. Her boyfriend, you know, murdered
Papa. We watched. My sister and me, we worked all the time. When the

stepdad wanted to plant a field, he had us move all the rocks. Big
rocks. Wrecked my feet, you know, 'cause I wore Sister's shoes. Never
fit. The stepdad used me. Yes, honey, raped me. Then Mama ran off.
We was sent to our Aunt and Uncle's, good people, yes, but hard.
Already had a bunch of kids. We all worked hard, inside and outside.
I left at 17 to go to Nurses' Training. Felt free those days. Met your
grandpa. We was married at 20, 1922. First thing he said was, "I'm
gonna wear the pants." I said, "I'm glad you're gonna wear your pants,
Ray." But I knew he hated how his Ma'd always wore the pants. So
that's the way it was. He wore the pants. Never knew what we had in
the bank. 53 years. He always made out like we was poor. So I had a
big garden, put up food for the winter. He liked canned fruit for
dessert, supper and dinner. Then when freezers come along, had two
freezers. When he died and I saw the bankbook, I like to died myself.
Had more money than I'd ever use if I lived to be 200. Sold that place
in three weeks. Never care to garden again. Nope.

III

    Trembling, Grandma holds my hand.
    We listen as doctors sling jargon,
    "ventricle enlargement, absorption
    mechanism, intermittent pressure,"
    nurses whisper euphemisms,
    "ready for intervention,
    intensive primary care."

The boardroom smells of Lemon Pledge
and rubbing alcohol; dust ribbons
through venetian blinds.
We're here to decide her fate.

Is it Alzheimer's?
Is it normal pressure hydrocephalus?
Is it senile dementia?

Trusting, she looks into my eyes.
"Why don't they just say I'm crazy
and let it go at that?"

Smiling, she eats her Chicken Medley.
I wonder if she's forgotten the meeting
we left just twenty minutes ago.
The restaurant booth is full of light,
red carnations in a table vase
spin as the waitress passes by.
I listen to lovers at the next table,
absently arrange her napkin
to catch a drip of gravy.

IV

Oh, hi, Doll! Welcome back! Since you left I haven't been so good. My
eyes is still tearing up all the time, can't read or nothing, no word yet

from the doctor about the operation. Guess someone has to die. Seem like Jack don't think I have half a brain. I did forget to go down to lunch one day, but they brought it up to me. Meat loaf. Oh, and I did another boo boo. Dressed to go to church on Tuesday, but I just changed my clothes back. My feet's killing me, but the shoes is some better. Did you talk to Walter? Letter last week said they was doing all right. Hot there. Hot as hell, Walter said. Wish they was closer. Must be hard for you to have your dad so far. Jack's gettin' the motor home ready for vacation. Probably needs a rest from me, huh?! Glad you're home. Don't know what I'd do without you. You're so good to me. Jack's a good boy, too, a good boy.

V

Warm
August afternoon.

We three,
my grandma, my daughter, and I,
are in the city's Rose Garden.

"Nothing smells better than warm roses,"
my daughter declares as she picks
newly fallen petals, holds handfuls
to Gram's nose, lays them in her lap –
lavender, pink, crimson, yellow, ivory.

Wheelchair tires spit gravel in the path.
White hair, warm to touch.

Gram the Queen,
lap full of petals,
leans into fragrance
and smiles.

One bush near the path,
salmon blossoms waving,
draws Grandma's cloudy eyes.
I push her closer.

She leans, pulls a stem
between long fingers close to her nose,
inhales, inhales again.

"I wonder," she sighs,
"if there'll be roses in heaven."

Bearing Witness
       - *for Maggy*

        In strength you speak your truth,
            exorcise the demon silence
              [no more secrets]*
     and we, encircling you, bear witness
              [you are safe]
        to your pain, his shame, her claim
         that "you were just too sensitive"
              [you are brave].
          Old violence and anger spew,
      erupt in bursts, but cannot burn you
              [you are safe]
your boundaries, which you and sisters guard, are firm
              [breathe].

      In clarity you separate your memory,
            explode the family myth
              [we're right here],
     shake the invisible rattle, take your turn,
     gather power, make transforming magic,
           crystallize the healing years
              [this is good]
      your exploration, excavation of the causes
          of the numbness, terror, shame
              [you're doing fine].
        Now you shine in power as you speak,
             and we bear witness
              [breathe].

*to be whispered

76

Mondi by Moonlight
- *for Meg*

Though I never saw her face,
watched her only through your words,
I knew Mondi
before she entered moonlight -

knew her wisdom -
her grasp that you had practiced deprivation,
had starved your woman self
to feed others' expectations,
her awareness that when, in your dream,
wildebeests circled round you rump to rump
before you went under the knife yourself,
they were the slain beasts from safaris
come back to be your companions
and I saw her total faith that you are on your path -

knew her love -
that when you'd said, "I cannot love the outcast
part of me,"
she had replied, "I can."
I witnessed all the times, year after year,
she mirrored your clear sight
into your need to love, to love without condition,
the radiance inside of you.
And that she called from Paris
when looking at the moon
was not enough.

In the Phoenix Pyre

Soul loss is regarded as the gravest diagnosis in [shamanism], being seen as a cause of illness and death. Yet it is not referred to at all in modern Western medical books.

- Jeanne Achterberg

This above all, to refuse to be a victim.

- Margaret Atwood, *Surfacing*

1

So, This Is Dying

"Something is terribly wrong
        in my head," I whisper to my
beloved at the end of the service
        on a January Sunday morning.
Boom! as I buckle between
        rows of chairs to the carpet,
I am tumbling into a tunnel
        long as the Mississippi River,
wavering ribbon of dark and light,
        river off whose banks ricochet
echoing voices and a silence
        longer than rivers of space, where
long ago Mama songs merge with
        voicelessness I cannot understand,

muffled sounds of love compete with
        mute howls - complete oblivion.

An ultimatum:
        Choose.
Choose the tunnel
        or
the voices.
        My choice,
but only one.

When I can think again,
        much later,
I remember the tunnel,
        the choice,
and I say, somewhere beyond
        the terror,
"So, this is dying."

But that January morning
        I do not think.
I lean out of the tunnel
        into the voices
and smell perfume
        above my head, the head
my friend holds in her lap.

A bandsaw of pain
        shrieks through my skull,
the head held in one woman's lap.
        The body attached to my head
jerks, shakes, trembles.
        I'm not sure I made
the right choice.

2

The Migraine Coloring Book

Page One: Color the vice grips
clamping the crown of your head,
the base of your neck and behind
your eyes purple, black, and red.
Thick handles, jagged tips tighten wide
bands. Press hard. The colors are deep.

Page Two: Color the electric waves
sizzling through your skull
burgundy, blue, and steel gray.
Make three slashing circuits - Bzzztt! -
around the top of your head like
a monk's tonsure, from the forehead to
the back of the skull like a granite band,
from the bridge of your nose to the back
of your neck like a hangman's noose ajar.

Page Three: Color the cones of fire,
entering your brain from your temporal
plates above your ears, the occipital ridge
above your neck, your temples, and your
eyes. Color them blood red, orange, maroon.
Streak ice blue through the centers of the cones –
the crayons must meld fire and ice.

Page Four: Color the lead ball, pulsing
ten shades of gray and black, heavy, hard.
Fill your brain with dirty fog that does not lift.
Send sparks of red, black, and blue out from
the ball in every direction. Make it 4th of July
inside of a cannon. Bear down. Break a crayon.
Make the picture last six months.

3

I cannot touch the terror

I cannot touch the terror,
the fear I feel
when the sap of my soul
drains out, as if I'm a maple
and it's winter in Vermont,

when the force of my spirit
is lost   as I fall,
blows away in a Miami
hurricane of pain

that threatens to suck everything
out of my skull,
and they cannot name the cause.

I cannot touch the terror

because it is too hot:
hot as the woodstove on baby fingers,
hot as the forest fire breaking the line,
hot as the burn after bombing a village,
hot as the fever that scares a nurse.

because it is too cold:
cold as a frozen pipe on the tongue,
cold as a river, tumbling over a rapid,
cold as Minnesota midnight, car
            stuck in a snowdrift,
cold as her eyes after I said "no."

because it is too sharp:
sharp as the razor across her wrist,
sharp as the knife clean through his thumb,
sharp as the teeth of a terrified jaguar,
sharp as sheet metal thrown by a twister.

because it is too hard to reach:
hard to reach as the man
            when I told him he'd hurt me,
hard to reach as a breach calf, perfect pitch,
hard to reach as the answers to my questions.

I clutch the terror
in my hand that will not close,
when I can't move without some help,
remember a movie I saw last week
or a poem I've had memorized for years.

I handle the terror,
my beloved does too,
every day the pain refuses to abate,
when the pressure of my blood
first plummets and then spikes,
and my soul holds to my body
by a filament of air.

But I cannot touch the terror,
and they cannot name the cause.

4

Trial By Physician
        - *for Sharon, co-survivor*

Emergency Room Physician:

"Oh, I'm sure she could open her eyes –
she just doesn't want to."

The pain peels the skin off my eyes,
careens through my skull like bank shots

on a pool table in a smoky, loud bar.
I ask my eyelid muscles to move,
but they will not obey.
I strain, I shake, I try, I fail.

Family Physician:

"It's just a little migraine, I'm sure.
Rest today. Go back to work tomorrow."

I cannot move alone, walk in slow motion,
fording deep rivers in winter, leaning on
strong arms, and only when I must.
I lie in darkness, see life in twos and threes
and in my skull grenades explode. Again. Again.

Family Physician:

"What!? She's supposed to be better!"

I soak in shame, shiver from the ice
of his judgment flung. I want to scream,
but fear the sound would kill me,
"What do you mean 'supposed'?"
I'm the woman you've called brilliant,
level headed, never given to hysterics
or neurotic fears. If I don't die
from this pain scouring out my skull,
will I die from not screaming?

Neurologist:

"Yes, there's definite weakness
all along your right side, and I see
you can't close your right hand.
But you're just not putting full effort
into making a fist."

How do you measure my effort?
How do you measure
the quiver in my arm from straining
to close my hand,
the sweat beading above my lip
and on my brow,
the lurching in my belly?
How do you measure my rage?

Neuro-opthamologist:

"My tests reveal no *physical* reason
for your distress."

I see every word, face, flower, or pen
multiplied two or three times before me,
so I cannot read or write.
I am a reader and writer by trade.
I cannot work.

Your machines, scopes, and lenses
find no reason for this "distress."
You believe them, blame me.

Do you think I've never heard the word
'psychosomatic'?
Doctor of the eyes, behind your machines,
who do you see when you look at me?

Internist:

"I don't like this at all.
This blood pressure is completely erratic."

She asks me to stand up.
Blood pressure plummets.
She tells me to lie down.
Blood pressure rockets.

I vomit. I can't sleep,
don't know days from nights.
forget who's called,
what or when I ate.
And the migraine never recedes.
Sharon and I speak of death.

Three months.
Fifteen specialists.
Fifty tests.
I finally ask, "In how many cases
do you never reach a diagnosis?"
I watch her shake her head behind the chart,
"About 50%."

Internist:

"If you insist on getting another opinion,
I'd suggest you see a psychiatrist."

I sit in the parking lot sobbing.
Beneath the wounds, bruises spread,
I have been pummeled, thwacked,
though my attackers do not see my face.
"Before this," I tell my beloved,
"I have never known despair."

She rubs my freezing hands, says,
"Don't forget who you are.
I won't let you forget who you are."

I whisper, "I will never go back.
They have no idea what they do not know."

5

Diagnosis

It might have been a
microscopic lacunar infarction,
a teensy stroke on a back left spot in the brain,
or it might have been a
transcient ischemic attack,
or it might have been
a drop attack,
the sort that's common with
chronic fatigue immune dysfunction syndrome,

or it might have been some,
or it might have been none.
It might have been God
in a bolt of lightning
to get my attention.
But I wasn't on the road to Damascus,
I wasn't quite blinded,
and it took me awhile to get the message.

6

I need to tell you

I need to tell you
        what I learned,
what I learned when the
        taste of pain
was acid and ash
        in my mouth,
in the mouth of my mind
        from morning to night
for months.

I need to tell you
        how I learned to turn
that taste to sweetness
        by reciting a list,
each day the list plus one,
        making myself remember –

focusing, repeating, adding,
    repeating the list,
each day the list plus one –
    to forget the pain,
a list of what I'd miss most
    if I died.

I need to tell you
    that I learned that gratitude,
a litany of thanks,
    the act of savoring the taste
of who and what I love,
    was healing balm.
It was the only drug I took.

And now I need to tell you
    what I'll miss most when I die:
my beloved's smile and neck and knee,
    Mozart on a Sunday morning,
crème brulée, a chickadee,
    my sister's unmistakable guffaw–

the feel of paint on canvas,
    splotches, bumps, swirls, and splashes,
the sight of lightning slashing
    across a charcoal sky,
finding agates, seagulls flying,
    wearing silk and jeans–

sorting through our wedding bundle,
    knowing Mama wants to hear,

fishing beside the McKenzie with Dad,
     picking raspberries at dawn,
smelling sandalwood and daphne,
     and stroking Brindle's fur –
crawfish with remoulade,
     time to watch my children grow,
asking questions,
     friends I trust with all of me,
the smell of a campfire,
     coffee with cream –

No matter when I leave,
     I know my list will be long,
each day the list plus one,
     and I will never, no matter when,
have had my fill
     of family around my table,
stepping off a train,
     Christmas trees and candles,
or a pen in my hand.

7

For St. Jude, The Shaman
     – *thank you, Dr. Paul*

"Your illness is not psychosomatic,"
you said. "You have been betrayed.
You have clearly suffered serious trauma
to the brain, and you can heal. I can help."

The room shimmers.
Your eyes are not guarded.
You never look away.
I call you St. Jude.
You take on hopeless cases.
You stand before me,
the first medical man or woman
who breaks the mold.
You, with your Mayo Clinic degree,
have not lost your curiosity –
you are the only one I've found.

You do the Shaman's work,
clear my soul's path to find its way home,
back into my body once again.

"Once the medicos get the motion sensitive
M.R.I. out of the lab, they'll apologize to you.
Their technology wasn't advanced enough
to tell them what listening hands could."

You touch me, trust your hands
to listen, and my body speaks of healing.
The room spins. And then it stays in place.

My heart swims on warm seas,
floats on waves of comfort, undulating ease
of being believed, seen, accompanied.
I begin to make plans for living.

8

Healing

happens in spirals,
        in circles, yes,
circles that grow wider,
        open, make more space

happens in spirals of skill,
        to assess, discern, intuit
and act   yes, skillful work
        that creates more space

happens in circles of wise ones,
        practicing Chi Kung, Tai Chi, yes,
giving acupuncture, massage, and cranial-sacral
        adjustments, revealing more space

happens in spirals, where
        full hearts meet brilliant minds, yes,
spin together to puzzle, ask and answer
        tough questions,   allow more space

Healing   happens
        in spirals
                yes   circles that open
                        spirals   make space

- With thanks to Vicki, Jennifer, Barbra, Joan, and Michelle

9

In The Phoenix Pyre

With charred and crumbling talon
   I sift through ash,
      touch the dust of who I used to be -
         splintered bone and crushed glass heart -
           wince when shards pierce through.

Amid the grey white dying,
   I find one coal,
      golden ember under crust of cold,
         and softly blow - whoo - ahh - whooo -
           smell the flame's heat spread.

From newborn passion,   longing,
   I sprout one wing,
      and then another, feathers - yearning
         to be free - fan like a rainbow,
           then   I fly,   I sing.

Leaves in the Shadows

When you lose a friend,
then find it wasn't a friend you lost,

look at the sky
until your throat, that rusty garden gate,
unlocks.

Look at the shadows
clouds make across the sky

above the apple orchard
while you breathe. Watch the shadows
and clouds

and sky and breath
until your eyes no longer burn.

And when your eyes don't burn
and your breath runs full as a
waterfall on a wild river,

sit still until
you are empty, open as a trail

into the wilderness,
until you love emptiness as much
as you loved the friend.

Let what was full,
the illusion and your love and your throat,

your eyes and the sky,
go empty as the woods beyond your window
sound at midnight,

drop silently into your breath,
that very one.

To practice loving the real,
paint particular trees - fir, hemlock, pine -
beneath the sky

and clouds and shadows
until you sketch

the possibilities flickering
in unoccupied presence - in what is
and is not - until you can see

maple leaves in the shadows of branches
when the tree is bare.

III:

HEALING THE WOMANHEART

crocus in the snow

after white desert of chill,
spiritwind bitter as smoke,
frozen winter of wandering,

you appeared again,
bright yellow,

a beginning, spring,
bursting "Yes!"

into the howling of change,
spiritbreath soft as a leaf,
tender summers of searching

Grace of Golden Weeping

I cannot heave my heart into my mouth.
    – Cordelia in *King Lear*

I'm kin to her when I, in pain, am mute,
exile myself into my room, take cello out and
heave my heart into my hands and ears and wrists,
ask it to sing my heart sound as I draw the bow

across its strings and find it resonant with truth.
Ear cocked toward its neck, I'm robin listening
for ear- not earth-vibrations, and soon the song arises,
grace sustained, vibrato making round the sound.

In due time I feel the warmth of fire through fog,
a caramel, golden weeping. Cradled at my shoulder
and between my legs, it calls me home, draws me close,
gives me voice to cry and speak and sing.

To Come Down Here

Moving,
rolling over and in
the shoulder, arm,
throat and belly
of my mother country,
taught me to love
water,
light,
and the color green.

Born on the border
of fern and fir,
sage and juniper,
in the shadow of seven
volcanic breasts,
I have spent half a life
falling to one side,
then the other –

one place: not enough light,
too much water,
plenty of green.
another: no water,
blinding light,
no green in long seasons –

to come down here
at canyon's edge beside a bay,
near ocean, rivers, lakes.
Light, often muted
in the morning,
filtering in shafts through
eucalyptus boughs,
splays open by noon,
sharp at water's edge.
And I see each day,
while hummingbirds hover,
a thousand shades of green.

Self-Portrait II

Questing, a woman dares to reinvent herself.
  – Dana Heller, *The Feminization*
  of Quest Romance

No more teacher clothes.
I want chamois shirts
and shorts with pockets I'll need
for a trek in the Himalayas.
I want a tutu and overalls for my
new career as a ballerina electrician,
a carpenter's apron and power tools
so I can work on Habitat for Humanity
and build my writing studio.

No more timidity, no cringing.
I can say "no" with grace
and my opinion about anything.
I don't need your approval
and I won't shrivel when you yell
or weep. I have limits, you know.
I will learn to climb sheer rocks,
fly a helicopter, handle bees
and embrace every dragon I meet.

Distance

And distance. Above all, a certain distance of the
mind and heart had been absolutely essential.
    - Paule Marshall, *Praisesong for the Widow*

Daughters,
take your distance.
Keep a space apart.
Give your jaguar minds
room to stretch,
your lion hearts
their sunny plain.

Do not let them
crowd you,
growl when you must.
Zookeepers cannot
remember the savannah.
Leap and bare your teeth,
let your muscles flex,
and yawn.

You know
the way home –
slow motion
in your leopard skin
through Himalayan light –
and you can lunge.

The Tastes of Sounds
  *- with thanks to Judith Barrington
   for Mar de Jade*

Dreaming of the tastes of sounds,
I find myself on the savannah,
listening to lullabies of swaying grass,
tasting vanilla, cinnamon and mint,
watching prides of lions twitch in time.

And when I wake at dawn,
hearing butterflies aquiver on my lashes,
tasting spindrift on my lips and tongue,
smelling café au lait and warm brioches,
I look for maverick messages in clouds.

At Waldport, Walking

The south wind hurries,
pushes me north, puffing,
motherrushing me in winter
to the yellow schoolbus.

Spindrift sprays my face,
yells a message, straining,
that I cannot understand
above the blue-white roar.

By the Lighthouse

I have come to write by the lighthouse.
Surfers glide on liquid silver far below.

The lighthouse cat slinks along the sill,
tiptoes over my shoulder, breast,
circles three times, makes a nest in my lap.
I cradle her fur like a hot cup of tea.
Our winter bones crave warmth.

She nibbles my pen and stretches
her golden arm across my journal.
The beacon shines in her eyes.
We both purr and blink,
she yawns, I scratch her chin.

Our bellies touching,
I let the pen fall.

Tilting

But the solitude that really counts is the solitude
of the heart; it is an inner quality or attitude that
does not depend on physical isolation.
                        - Henri Nouwen, *Reaching Out*

I like to drive toward the coast at dusk,
know I have that tilting cottage waiting,
say aloud the words inside my head
turning into phrases, lines of poems
as I push to break the city's bounds.

The ocean, molten lead beneath the moon,
outside the tilting window rolling,
soothes me - setting pencils in a row,
dictionary on my left, water on the right,
order just enough to calm the rush
of words so eager to be written down.

I write for days, my mind splayed out
in silence, save for tilting shutters creaking,
which satisfies the longings so completely
that I easily forget to eat more than
some rice cakes, cheese, and oranges
and sip my water or a cup of tea.

But my heart is always homesick
when I leave the tilting cottage, mourning,
until the words in me demand
that the ocean live in town.
So I pack the sand and spindrift,
bring the waves in poems home.

Honeysuckle

        A
honeysuckle vine
        climbs, winding
                on a wrought-iron trellis
        at each side of our front door.
Its green leaves, flowers
        white and yellow,
                twine,
        form an aromatic arch,
hinting at sweet wine
                inside.

        Bees that hum
                in summer,
busy storing yellow powder,
        sip nectar
                from the blooms,
        carry magic dust
from porch
        to hive that soon will drip
                with honey
        scented by these blossoms
                at our door.

To My Child
- *with thanks to M.A.K.*

My child, I'll listen with an open heart
    to all your hurt and hope,
your memories and longings,
    the surfacing of secrets long suppressed.

I'll share a belly roar with you
    as we clap back at seals and giggle at mallards
who laugh right back at us.

I'll skip in sand to keep the dance's time,
    go barefoot anywhere you choose,
eat candy canes and Cracker Jacks,
    sing and whistle in the car,
and throw my watch away.

When you weep all through the night,
    I'll hold you, head nuzzled at my neck,
and stroke your hair in silence until dawn.

My child, my daughter, sister, self,
    I'll watch with you in wonder as anemones
sift waves of water, salt, and sand
    for the nourishment they need,
as starfish cling to rocks, then fly, released,
    to grasp a rock again.

I'll ask "why?" and "how?" and "why not this?"
        to keep you company, and we'll fly kites
and talk to seagulls, terns, and cormorants
        who also catch the wind.

And when you rock in fear,
        the chair squeak echoing the past,
I'll never leave again,
        translate what you feel,
or talk the pain away.

You'll know one day what safety is,
        safety to the bone.
That day I'll see you soar,
        our bond as clear as breath
and just as soft.

Otters at Noon

Mother, all body and being,
nuzzles her nose in daughter's fur,
urges the pup toward wild surf's edge
and leaves her there to watch.
Mom slithers off sand into the salt,
undulates, plunges, stretches to surface,
breathes like trees, imperceptibly.

Otter, all body and being,
takes her daughter's neck in teeth,
eases her onto motherbelly,
floats on her back intent on pup,
lolling, lulling, paws protecting,
while waves slap over, wash away,
the two submerge, resurge.

Mother and daughter in water,
infused with body and being,
bobbing, darting,
stretching curves of fur
in the current of the day,
that watery light, and
this one wave.

Mother Me, Water Me
- for Sharifah, with thanks for Watsu and Water Dancing

Mother me,
water me,
whirl me,
swirl me,
pull me
through mother pool,
hold me and cradle me,
ladle me, curl me,
cuddle me, stretch me,
dip me,   flip me,
I breathe into places
I've never before –

Minnow me,
dolphin me,
seal me,
trout me,
I'll hold my breath
while you turn me to flow –

Funnel me,
tunnel me,
carry me home,
home to the water,
the womb water, tomb water,
re-womb me, Mother,
make room for me now –

Mother, oh mother me,
                hold me to breast
where our hearts can beat tandem,
                                rippling,   pulsing,
        in waters of wonder –

Slow me,
        float me,
                        surface me,
                                        still me,
my ears echo heart beat
                        and every cell tingles,
        I come back to harbor,
                        whole.

Reclamation
     - for Lynn

I see mauve beyond my eyelids,
soft light filtered through the blinds
as I lie naked, warm, and loosely wrapped.
I smell almonds of the tropics in the oil,
feel your hands pulse healing heat
as they pull and knead my flesh,
stretch the space in which I breathe,
tune my worn and tired muscles into song.
I hear whales sing lullabies through waves,
while, beneath your touch, I find safety and
my power to claim the earth of me –
my sky, my fire and ocean –
and the whales sing, swimming
through my body, in my blood.

September Morning

Meditating
    one September morning
she hears her breath
    breathing
letting in –
    letting out –
        letting be –
Stellar jay squawking
    letting in –
757 taking off from the airport
        letting out –
tea water bubbling in the kettle
            letting be –
car tires skimming the freeway
    of her breath
breathing.

You come into my mind

when the Met broadcast comes on the radio,
or someone cries as a marching band passes by,

when "Amahl" and the visitors arrive at Christmas,
or Linda Ronstadt sings "Blue Bayou,"

when someone mentions mayonnaise,
bratwurst or crème caramel,

when I see a cocker spaniel
or pet a Siamese cat,

when I read Joan Sutherland retired
or Pavarotti cancelled again somewhere,

when I light the first fall fire,
set a turkey roasting, or read by campfire glow,

when someone chews a fine red wine
or carries the new book to lunch for weeks.

For Marilyn

Reading to the Cooks
        - for the cooks at Flight of the Mind,
        1990-1992

All my life I've read in kitchens.
I read to women cooking now
like a child returning home from school.

Slicing peaches, washing dishes,
chopping peppers, mixing dough,
they listen, eyes and hands absorbed.

I recite the newest poems,
fill up on sounds of kitchen
and watch them eat my words.

At lunch I look for poems in the salad
and hear my mother whistling "Stardust"
as she stands at the sink shelling peas.

Skyline

- for Vicki

Shade
after sun
is like forgiveness –
you don't appreciate it
until you need it.

In sun and shade
we walk,
stretch,
you coach,
I circle my shoulders,
plant my feet,
practice Chi Kung.
We swing our arms,
reach them toward clouds,
sit back to back
and sing the sounds of earth,
sniff autumn scents of bay and pine,
their varied greens against the golden hills.

Slowly,
slowly,
up
and
down
the trail,

I walk,
sing,
stretch
and still my soul
in sun and then in shade.
And as I scan the skyline and you,
my body forgives my mind's long absence.

The Heart Labyrinth
    - for Jen

"What's the deal with these rocks?"
shouts the kid in the Notre Dame shirt.
His arm slung around a girl's shoulder,

he peers over the cliff to the labyrinth
shaped like a heart, through which
we three women walk in silence,

slowly, as if we are in a cathedral.
We are here to meditate under the sun,
to consider the path to the Heart.

Approaching the labyrinth, I had balked,
afraid of the steep cliff, believing I'd fall,
when my friend said firmly, "I'm not afraid.

Put your hands on my shoulders,
look at your feet. And take baby steps."
I took my steps, looked at my feet

and waited for the hard part.
"We're here," she whispered. I smiled.
One leads, then follows, the labyrinth flows.

We pace in the welcome March sun.
"The beauty of the labyrinth," my friend explains,
"is that there's no right way. The way you go

is the way. That's the beauty of it."
That's when the boy yells. He doesn't really
want to know the answer to his question.

I want to scream at the Notre Dame boy,
"These rocks show the way to the Heart!"
But instead I pray for the Notre Dame boy,

that Notre Dame boy and his girl:
"Put your hands on my shoulders, look at your feet.
Just take baby steps. . . . We're here."

Visitors

Ruby throat,
　　　racing heart,
　　　　　　whirring wings
and I
　　　find nectar,
　　　　　　sweet sanctuary
in the place
　　　where zinnias grow.
Color of life
　　　invites impatiens,
　　　　　　dahlias,
laughter
　　　and just enough
stillness.
Test flights,
　　　trust grows.
　　　　　　We both know
we're safe there
　　　to drink our fill.

Womanrites
      - for Sharon

We sat together, naked, in the late afternoon light,
        eating pasta salad from one bowl with two forks,
        planning lives;
We sipped fine, strong coffee at dawn, sharing dreams,
        extending solitary night wanderings,
        alone no more;
We lounged like lizards in the September sun, silent,
        on the warm river rocks, savoring ourselves, the season,
        shared solitudes;
We cooked for friends, punctuating stories and directions
        with smiles and pats,
        stealing chopped vegetables;
We sudsed each other in the shower,
        singing in two different keys, bathed in candlelight
        and the gift of enough time;
We made birthdays unforgettable, full of delights
        for taste, touch, eyes, ears, memories that grew
        as years gathered;
We walked on the beach, forest trails, alpine meadows,
        exploring inner children, wise crones,
        and the Mother.

We've woven from these rites a life,
        marked with all these rites our days,
        spun a past to lay our future on.

Valentine

When
      you walk
            into the room

I stop breathing
      like a woman
            blind from birth
                  just given sight.

Beyond you
      the sun sets
            through linden leaves.

You,
      the sun,
            the leaves
                sway

to some silent jazz,
      shimmer
            like gold foil.

After a Coven of Years

After a coven of years
we are,
like the calla lilies
before you now,
ever unfolding,
light shimmering on surfaces
just discovered and surveyed,
opening to the sun,
the daily miracle,
again and again and again,
of love's warming.

To Make A Home
  - *for Ami and Jesse, on their wedding day*

To make a home
at first   seems no big trick:
buy a futon, hang a poster, get a phone.
But, after while
the props reveal themselves
to be just that: props,
and not the thing itself,
not home.

To make a home
takes tools
no hardware store can sell.
You know them, son and daughter,
you use them now with skill.
You talk and listen
with hearts open wide,
mountaineers
who trust your ropes
through peak and dark abyss.
You know the blessing
of caress,
the healing in warm eyes.

Keep your tools sharp
with solitude
as with togetherness.
Make rituals in every room

with food, the songs you sing,
and stories told: keep watch
for mystery to unfold.

Always leave room
to make your circle wider:
Your home is a host.
And grow your garden:
The basil grown this year
will be the stuff of legends.

To make a home
takes time.
Five years and more
have brought you here,
daughter, son,
woman, man.
And now we wish you lifetimes,
vintage years,
to make a home.
You can do no nobler work.
It is for good reason
there is a word for home
in every language.

From the Mountains
- for Jennifer, at 50

Fifty spirals through
summers, autumns, winters, springs
shine in your smile today,
carved tracks
you've made through yearn and stretch
call to your heart in dreams.

Sierra, Trinities, Marbles, Cascades,
your soul gathers strength from the mountains.

The muscles of
your tan bare legs and back and arms
remember a thousand trails,
forged streams,
your eyes gleam with reflections
of moons over mountain lakes.

Sierra, Trinities, Marbles, Cascades,
your body is fed by the mountains.

The granite and shale,
cedar, juniper, pine,
give you brave bones,
brisk blood,
the winds whip up your courage,
your passion to make the earth just.

Sierra, Trinities, Marbles, Cascades,
your vigor is forged in the mountains.

The knowledge you
carry in that backpack of your brain
changes lives.
The questions you
live with when you slip or fall
inspire as well. Everything is of use.

Sierra, Trinities, Marbles, Cascades,
your mind becomes vast like the mountains.

Stone, Water, Circle

Earth-filled stone
we pass around
and fill it
with our pain.
Hands conduct
the memory's hurt,
the heart's heat.
We hold
each other's pain,
then pass it on.

Stone, water, circle.

Pain-filled stone,
the pitcher pours
clear water
over, through the pain,
releasing pain,
cleansing rain.
We dry the stone.

Stone, water, circle.

Love-filled stone,
our hands pour
energy
through, into the rock,

receiving love,
breathing love.
The stone breathes love.

Stone, water, circle.

I am, you are the stone.
I am, you are the water.
I am, you are the circle.

Stone, water, circle.

Haiku by Heart
   - for Pema and Yeshe

Ants, grasshoppers, flies,
flickers and warblers in pines,
stillness in motion.

Fire circles and walks,
cold stars and warm canyon walls.
The wonder goes deep.

Circles

A Performance Piece for Seven Female Voices

Voice 1: One woman
Voice 2: in a circle
Voice 3: reveals fresh wounds
Voice 4: or old scars newly torn
Voice 5: in raw words
Voice 6: or silence,
Voice 7: lays her pain open
Voice 1: in air.
Voice 2: Another exposes
Voice 3: need bare as desert bone,
Voice 4: longing red as lungs.
Voice 5: Those whose voice
Voice 6: is still strangled
Voice 7: thank her
Voice 1: whose tongue has healed.
Voice 2: Women lean forward,
Voice 3: find a tissue, caress,
Voice 4: wipe wet hair out of eyes,
Voice 5: and do not look away.
Voice 6: Sisters make sounds
Voice 7: soft as rabbit's pelt.
Voice 1: Pain pulses,
Voice 2: undulates,
Voice 3: flickers into laughter
Voice 4: through mere touch

Voice 5: or wry quip,
Voice 6: then flashes into love
Voice 7: as soul flames glow
Voice 1: in circles.

Healing the Womanheart

Every week we make our circle,
        five years now,
wait through the seasons
        of our struggles to be free.
I look you in the eye, we can walk
        the fearfire path;
you face me, unafraid, then we stalk
        the angerholds.
We hear your fifty year old secret
        through the wail,
held until this moment
        in shame that is not yours
and we cheer each time one spies
        a spot of light, triumph palpable
through agony in tears.

Healing the womanheart
        takes time, takes time,
healing the womanheart
        takes time.

Every week we forge a safety ring,
        strong now, and in this sacred
crucible we all are changed;
        our honest labor pushes us
past all our walls,
        we reawaken wonder in our

jaded, wounded hearts
        as we watch each woman
heal her treasured pain,
        risk to release old myths,
obsolete life lies.
        We learn sounds to sing ourselves
to strength, lullaby the ships to harbor,
        hurts to wholeness,
chant our poisoned cygnets
        into powerful swans.

Healing the womanheart
        takes time, takes time,
healing the womanheart
        takes time.

Every week we make more space,
        needed now
For women bigger than we've been,
        as we become.
We challenge bankrupt patterns,
        intervene, call up courage
to dispute the claim, "I can't,"
        and with every new "I can!"
we shout shared joy.
        We also hold each other's
anguish in our arms,

bringing comfort, long awaited,
to the child who's known deeply
       for a lifetime what she needs,
but has not been safe to ask
       until right now.

Healing the womanheart
       takes time, takes time,
healing the womanheart
       takes time.

In That Cave

A Ritual Piece for Voice, Dance, and Drum

Hold me when I howl
in that cave, in that womb
of a room in the rock
by the ocean, to the motion
of the tides

while the waves
curl and eddy at our feet.

Join me in a chant
in that cave, in that hollow
we will hallow with our praise
by the water, we the daughters
of the moon

while the gulls
shriek and circle in the sky.

Tell me what you will
in that cave, in that round,
and the sound of the sand
will caress, also bless
through the breeze

while the walls
hum and echo ancient charms.

Dance with me tonight
in that cave, in that ring,
we will sing with our bodies
exultation, our elation
in the dark

while the stars
burn and flicker in our eyes.

Praying for Release

Autumn,

urge me to drop
every leaf I don't need –
every task or habit I repeat
past its season,
every sorrow I rehearse,
each unfulfilled hope I recall,
every person or possession
to which I cling –
until my branches are bare,
until I hold fast
to nothing.

Blow me about
in your wild iron sky,
crush
all that's puffed up,
fluff
all that in me needs
to go to seed,
send my shadows to sleep.

Tutor me
through straining night winds
in the passion of moan and pant,
the gift of letting go

at the moment
of most abundance -
in the way of
falling apples, figs, maple leaves, pecans.

Open my eyes
to your languid light,
let me stare in your face
until I see no difference
between soar and fall
until I recognize
eternity
in single breaths,
faint whispers of cool air
through lungs.

Show me the way
of dying
in glorious boldness -
yellow, gold, orange, rust, red, burgundy, brown.

Praying for a Thaw

Winter,

sing me a symphony
in wind,
drum whole notes of rain
on my head.

Shake me
through the fog of sleep,
rock me to the rhythm
of my own true pulse.
Flood me
with your holy water,
make me
gasp for breath.

Speak to me
in a language of diamonds,
single drops of rain
in sunlight.
And I will respond
from my watery depths,
flowering, shining.

Wake me
to worship my garden.
I will follow the pace
of filtered light,

discover a new rainbow,
this one white, beige, brown, gray, black.
I want to dance with skeletons,
wet, bare limbs and hips,
recite, over and over,
moon chants I learn in my sleep
through long night mists and storms.

Whisper to me
the cleansing secret
of torrent and gale,
drench me
and pull at my roots.

Carry me away
on your fierce sky music,
whirl me in the current
of raging rivers,
foamy waves.

Teach me to dream
hot life blood
into my cold fingers.
Call me
with your cool tongue,
and I will reply with fire.

Praying to Break Through

Spring,

wake me to grow,
stretch and tremble,
break up my clay,
crumble me fine.
Warm all my rows,
the hills and furrow paths,
as you work me, wet or dry.

Send for me, soft,
in the language
of lambs' tongues,
velvet oh's and ah's.
And I will come out
from my winter-slowed cave,
whispering, aching.

Push me through
steaming earth, rich loam,
stir my roots deep
from beneath.
Quicken my core
with your hot hands, and
I will sing spirals of seeds.

Heave me up
into the sun,
pull me to the surface
by my pale green shoots.
Shout your YES!
into my bulbs,
fill my limbs with light.

Pour me into
the fragrance of change,
make me fertile and strong.
Open my fists
of tightly furled petals
into the glory of
white - green - pink - red.

Feed me full
of the promise of bloom,
take all of me you need.
Train me by tendril
to grow, grow still. I want
to learn your cycle by cell:
want - need - must - will.

Praying to Bear Fruit

Summer,

shine on my breasts,
in my hair, down my back
with the hot blue juice of your sky.
From earliest morning to late-coming night
may you boil, roil
in the blood
'til you burn all away
but perfume.

In soft night come close,
wet the garden
and field with my sweat,
the sap of bent back and knee
and the dew from
just enough cloud.
I want to wake
to breezes bursting with
tomato, marigold, mint, peony, basil,
geranium and dill.

Fill the forests, the mountains,
the lakes and the plains
with your
honey gold heat
to warm all wanderers,
wheat to see the pilgrims through
from harvest to bloom.

Nourish the babies,
old women and men
and the swaggering, sweltering youth
with your bounty,
a miracle
of just three moons.
Teach, if you will, delight by mouth,
utter joy of suck and chew and gulp
of the just right ripe.
And may we all bear fruit.

Pierce the earth
with primary colors –
blazing red, yellow, blue and green –
and lazy shades
of dawn and dusk –
moss, cornflower, pink, lavender, melon.
In your silent puncture,
pulsing,
heal us to the heart.

Let us,
oh, get us
to leap,   sing,   laugh,
and lie in the grass,
fall to our knees,
and turn somersaults
in your gleaming,
streaming
light.

ADVANCE PRAISE FOR THIS COLLECTION:

The lyrical magic and emotional resonance of Monza Naff's poems in
Healing the Womanheart *have caused me, as a lover and scholar of
poetry, to return to them again and again. Her precision of language and
image in evoking the natural world has helped me to retrieve a sense of
the sacred in my life. Her homages to the women she has held dear – her
grandmothers, her lovers past and present, the members of her support group
– transcend the private and rank among the best feminist lyrical tributes
I have read. Her ritual pieces are equally moving when read aloud to one's
self at home and when performed publicly and multivocally. These are poems
of compassion, solidarity, and survival; these are poems that women long
to read.*

     Mary K. DeShazer, Ph.D.
     Professor of Women's Studies and English, Wake Forest University

...Confessional poetry has been popular in this century, but **Healing the
Womanheart** *is confessional poetry with a difference. These poems have
their share of pain and anger, but unlike other contemporary poets, Monza
Naff assumes healing is possible and shows it occurring.*

     Marjorie D. Lewis, Ph.D.
     Professor Emeritus, Texas Christian University

*Adrienne Rich, in her essay "When We Dead Awaken: Writing as Re-Vision,"
urges women poets to speak "to and of women... out of a newly released
courage to name, to love each other, to share risk and grief and celebration."
Monza Naff is one of the few poets I know who has been able to bring together
in one volume that essential movement from pain through healing to the
four prayers of sheer exaltation at the end.* **Healing the Womanheart**
*is a mature, a composted book into which Monza has worked the gleanings
of a lifetime.*

     Mara Faulkner, OSB, Ph.D.
     Associate Professor of English, College of St. Benedict

*...**Healing the Womanheart** is a warm and generous collection, celebratory, sympathetic, and infused with a love not only for the real people in its pages but also for the real world – its flora, fauna, landscapes and seasons – she invites us to live in. Who could refuse?*

Mimi Khalvati
Director of The Poetry School in London

Monza Naff swings with ease between the red-tailed hawk on the fence post and her own debilitating period of illness, making potent and moving poetry from both. She gracefully crafts ritual song, designed to be useful in the world, as well as solitary meditation, always speaking of and from a generous heart. These are poems concerned with the spirit. Although they never cringe from painful or difficult truths, they leave the reader feeling hopeful and well nourished.

Judith Barrington
Co-Founder of Flight of the Mind and Soapstone

Also published by *Wyatt-MacKenzie Publishing*:

Monza Naff's ***Exultation: A Poem Cycle in Celebration of the Seasons***

Artwork by Katherine Witteman
Calligraphy by Carol Erickson DuBosch

ISBN 0-9673025-1-X

Price: $12.95 + *Shipping & Handling*

Healing the Womanheart is available on audiotape with the poet reading selections from this collection.

Price: $10.95 + *Shipping & Handling*

TO ORDER:

Contact IGS, or call the Publisher toll-free at 877-900-9626
or order ONLINE at *www.WyMacPublishing.com*

4100-10 Redwood Rd., #316, Oakland, CA 94619

510-336-0449 *Fax*: 510-336-0450
e-mail: MonzaNaff@aol.com

Classes, workshops, and retreats in meditation and
writing, spiritual formation and ritual making.